SWING EASY, HIT HARD

SWING EASY, HIT HARD

by Julius Boros

WITH OVER 100 ILLUSTRATIONS BY
LEALAND GUSTAVSON

INTRODUCTION BY GEORGE BAYER

Reprinted 1981

Published by Cornerstone Library
A Simon & Schuster Division of
Gulf & Western Corporation
Simon & Schuster Building
1230 Avenue of the Americas
New York, New York 10020

CORNERSTONE LIBRARY and colophon are
trademarks of Simon & Schuster, registered in
the U.S. Patent and Trademark Office.

This new Cornerstone Library edition is published by arrangement
with Harper & Row, Publishers Incorporated and is a complete and
unabridged reprint of the original hardcover edition.

Manufactured in the United States of America

ISBN 0-346-12305-4

To GOLFERS EVERYWHERE *who believe that good form and smooth swinging will produce lower scores and more enjoyable golf*

Twice Winner, National Open, 1952, 1963
Twice Winner, World Championship, 1952, 1955
Twice Leading Money Winner, 1952, 1955
Winner, PGA Golfer of the Year, 1952, 1963
Member, Ryder Cup Team, 1959, 1963
Twice Winner, Colonial National Invitational, 1960, 1963
Winner, Buick Open, 1963
Winner, Carling Open, 1958
Winner, Greensboro Open, 1964
Winner, Phoenix, Florida Citrus, Buick, 1967
Winner, PGA Championship, Westchester Classic, 1968
Lost in Playoff, Westchester Classic, 1975
Winner, PGA Seniors', 1971, 1977
Winner, Legends of Golf, 1979, J. Boros/R. DeVicenzo

Contents

SWING EASY, HIT HARD

Introduction

It is a great pleasure for me to write this introduction. In my years of traveling with Julius Boros, I have had untold opportunities to observe the manner in which he approaches golf and life. Everything he does shows a deliberate and conscientious effort, and yet he remains completely relaxed and seemingly imperturbable. His unassuming ways have gained him many friends; I know this book will add many more.

As a golfer, Julie has always believed that good form and a smooth swing will produce the greatest and the most consistent pros. But, more important, it is possibly the only way weekend golfers can play really good golf over an extended period of time. It is Julie's hope that more young golfers will realize this as they begin to shape their games.

Obviously, there is no one more qualified to write a book entitled *Swing Easy, Hit Hard* than Julie Boros. Besides his enviable record, his relaxed swing has been at least the next most noteworthy aspect of his golfing fame. When people see him play, they want to play the way he does. They sense that here truly is the uncomplicated way to play this game. Now everyone can learn to play the Boros way. In this book he has set down not only the basics of the golf swing but a whole philosophy for relaxed yet effective golf.

It has been a rewarding experience to have been so closely associated with Julie in the past. I feel sure that even at middle age he will continue to be one of the top players for many more years. I say that not only for myself but for the many friends who know him as a golfer and a person.

GEORGE BAYER

Part I:

Why the Mechanics
of the Golf Swing
Are Important

Chapter 1

THE SECRET OF BETTER GOLF

People often ask me, "How do you hit the ball so far when you swing so easy?" The answer is simple. I hit hard. Notice I didn't say I swing hard. The distance your ball travels is governed solely by the amount of power you unleash at impact. Having, like most pros, a *basic understanding* of how to do this, it becomes natural to "swing easy and hit hard." Remember the line that goes, "A little learning is a dangerous thing." Well that applies to golf as to most other endeavors in life. You can't play golf well unless you know the right movements and why these movements will contribute to a sound swing. You immediately handicap yourself on the course with less. It's like taking a car out on the highway when all you know about driving is how to start the car.

The purpose of this book is to give everyone a basic understanding of the correct golf swing (one that delivers maximum power), and of why your ball slices, hooks or flies straight. We'll dissect each element of the swing and I'll show you what they do and where they fit. Understand each part as we go along and picture it. Better yet, actually perform it with a club, so you'll know its place in the over-all swing. If you follow this advice, by the end of the book, even with just a little work, you'll be rewarded with lower scores, a greater enjoyment of the game and probably winning that 50¢ or $1 Nassau more frequently. This applies to everyone.

Try to think of your golf swing as an efficient machine. Each part of it is dependent upon the other parts; if one part is functioning incorrectly the others will be affected. But working together they deliver the same effective result time after time. This is your objective. Build the most efficient machine you can. You'll be surprised how much more enjoyable the game will be if you do.

Chapter 2

ON MEETING THE BALL

The action of the ball is the culmination of everything you have done up to the point of impact. It either goes where you meant it to or it doesn't and in either case you should know why. Controlling the action of the ball is the ultimate aim of the golfer. Don't forget, as obvious as this may sound, that the object of golf is to get the ball into the hole in as few strokes as possible. This can only be done when you've learned to control the ball. There is a period of time when, if the ball is correctly hit, it momentarily adheres to the face of the club. You'll never actually see this because you'll be swinging too fast when it happens, but I'm sure most of you have seen pictures of it. That instant of impact determines everything. To use a cliché, it's the moment of truth. You should predetermine the exact flight of the ball as to direction, distance, spin and loft. A straight shot is produced by bringing the club into the ball square to the line and swinging straight forward on the line. This is your objective and it isn't as hard as it sounds.

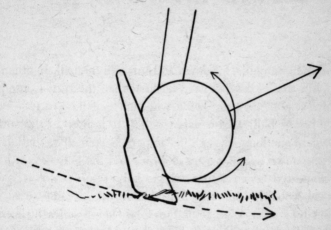

On every full shot, the ball momentarily adheres to the face of the club.

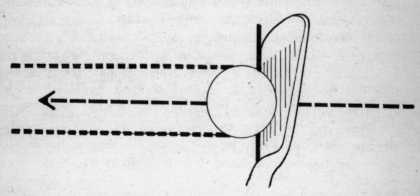

Straight shot: The clubface comes in straight and at a right angle (square) to the line of flight at impact.

Impact with the irons

For all the iron clubs, hit down and through the ball. In other words, your club should contact the ball first, then the turf. Consequently, the lowest point in your swing will be a half inch to two inches in front of your ball. This causes the ball to adhere to the surface of your clubface long enough to impart a spin. The ball is being squeezed down between your clubface and the grass beneath it. The spin imparted is an underspin, usually referred to as backspin. (You've probably seen this most beautifully demonstrated by the pros on television. Watch for the shots which sail a little past the cup and spin back to the hole. This is backspin at its best.) Backspin not only affects the ball when it lands but also in flight. When backspin has been applied the ball bores through the air more accurately. Should long grass, leaves or clover get between the ball and the clubface, the friction or spin will be lost. It's as if the club were greased. When this happens the ball will sail with little or no backspin. (When this happens, the pros say, "The ball flies.") For this reason I prefer to play my iron shots from a close cut fairway or even a bare spot, because I can get better stopping action on my ball from this kind of lie. In other words there isn't any grass or clover to get between my ball and the club. Finally, by the time the sole of your club has gotten down to the turf the ball is already airborne, rising at the angle dictated by the loft of the club. The loft of the club takes care of the angle of flight all by itself.

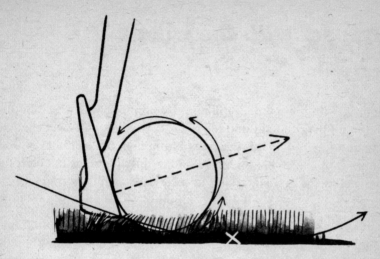

Impact with an iron: The club goes down and through the ball, creating backspin.

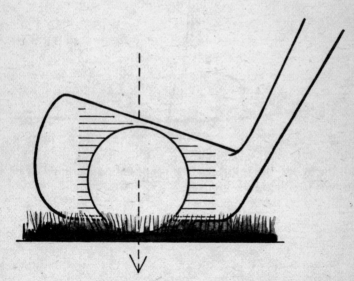

Correct contact with the center of the club.

Impact with the woods

Impact with the woods is different from impact with irons. Because you want the ball to fly and roll as far as possible, you must eliminate the backspin. To do this you must hit through the ball but not down on it. Thus the ball is contacted on the upswing or as the club runs parallel to the ground, giving us a forward or rolling spin.

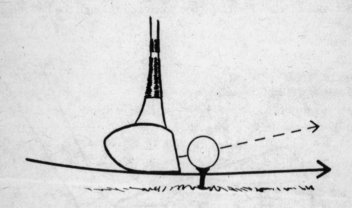

With the driver, the ball should be contacted on the upswing or as the club runs parallel to the ground.

Sidespins

If at the point of impact, your clubface is drawing across the ball in either direction it will impart a sidespin causing a hook or a slice. This applies to both woods and irons. A slice is caused by a clockwise spin being delivered on the ball. So long as the forward impetus is sufficient the ball travels on a nearly straight line. As the forward speed lessens, the sidespin bites into the air pulling the ball into the curve to the right. The faster the spin the more pronounced the curve. The same is true for the hook. The difference lies in the direction of the spin. The hook spins counterclockwise, thus curving to the left.

The pushed ball, which flies off line to the right, does not spin; it was hit in that direction by the angle of the clubface at impact. A push will generally fly in a straight line to the right; whereas the slice starts straight and then curves. The pulled ball, which is like the push although it flies to the left, is again the fault of the angle of the clubface at impact. Lastly we have the topped shot, caused by the club striking the ball above its middle half or just below the middle with the leading edge of the club.

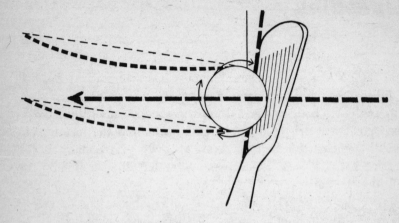

Clubface opened at impact. Result: a push or a slice.

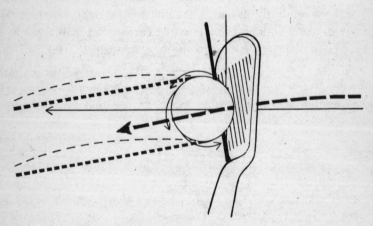

Clubface closed at impact. Result: a pull or a hook.

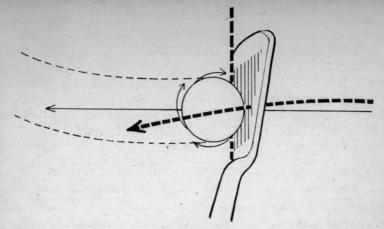

Fade impact.

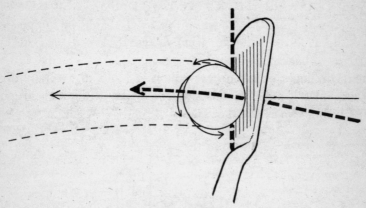

Draw impact.

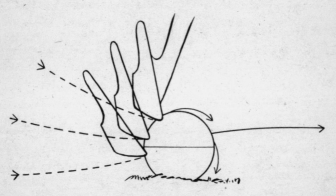

The topped shot.

Wind and spin

Hitting against a wind accentuates the spinning action on the ball in all directions. Slices and hooks curve more and faster. By this same reasoning a hard hit ball with crisp backspin will sometimes climb higher in the air than usual and may drop short of the target. When hitting any shot against the wind I use a longer club, shorten up on my grip a little, hit a bit easier and let the wind stop the ball. The desire to hit harder against the wind should be suppressed. Swing normally. A following wind materially lessens the effect of all spins, so backspin cannot be expected to be as effective in controlling the flight or roll of the ball. Your ball will naturally carry farther and roll more. In this situation I play a shorter and more lofted club and play the shot higher.

Chapter 3

STANCE: YOUR STRONG FOUNDATION

Now we've come to the first step in building an effective swing—stance. The first step in most anything you do involves the basics or fundamentals which when mastered make the other steps easier. So it is with golf. A good stance is the firm foundation upon which we will shape and mold your new, competent swing.

What is stance? It is the proper placing of your feet in relation to the line of flight you have selected to the target. Let's examine the three different stances and see what each will do.

Square stance

This is the basic stance from which the other two are adapted. The square stance should be your stance to hit a straight shot with your woods and long irons (one-, two- and three-). To adopt it, simply place your feet shoulder length apart, as measured from the inner edges of your shoes, touching the line. In all of these stances your left foot should be turned outward, toward the target, about 10 to 15 degrees, your right foot less. This facilitates an easier body turn and contributes to greater balance throughout the swing.

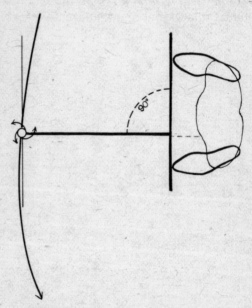

Place both feet touching the line. This is your stance for the woods and long irons.

Open stance

Move your right foot ahead of the line not more than four inches and your left foot slightly back. Use this stance for your medium (four-, five-, six-) and short (seven-, eight-, nine- and wedge) irons. As you progress from the medium to the short irons, your feet move closer together and your stance opens more.

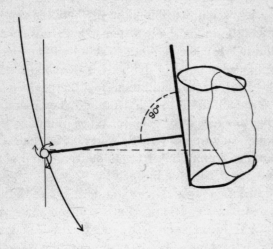

Move your right foot a few inches forward of the line and your left slightly back. In effect this moves your ball "forward." Your feet draw closer together as the length of the shot becomes shorter.

Closed stance

Drop your right foot behind the line two to four inches. Your left foot remains touching the line. Avoid using this stance until you can consistently hit a straight ball. The pros and expert amateurs use it mainly to produce a hook.

Obviously, stance has another role: that of providing the player with balance. Your swing must be a smooth, functional one-piece movement from beginning to end. To achieve this, you must be in balance throughout the swing. If you're off balance in some part of the swing, you've irrevocably lost some control, and control—the control *you* should have over your swing—is what we're shooting at. The first step to proper balance is to place your feet firmly on the ground with your weight distributed evenly between the balls and heels of your feet. If you have a tendency to lean forward onto your toes during the swing, make an effort to stay back on your heels.

The sideway balance point of the body is the hollow at the base of your throat. Note in the illustration how the center of balance changes as you shift from left to right. It is important that during the swing you have this feeling of balance. When you have built your successful swing, you won't have to worry about balance, you'll have it. It stands to reason that if you're delivering the same result time after time you must be in balance.

You've all heard the remark, "Keep your head still." All this means is stay in balance. The simplest rule I can give you about your head is forget it. If you're swinging properly, your head will be moving the little bit which is necessary. Let it move naturally. It will if you don't think about it.

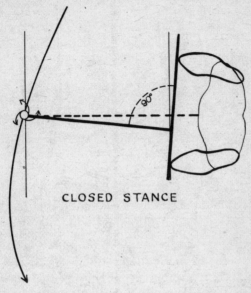

CLOSED STANCE

Drop your right foot behind the line about two to four inches. In effect this moves your ball "back." This stance accentuates the possibilities of a hook; don't use it until you can handle it. For both the open and the closed stances, your hands remain in nearly the same position relative to your body and left foot.

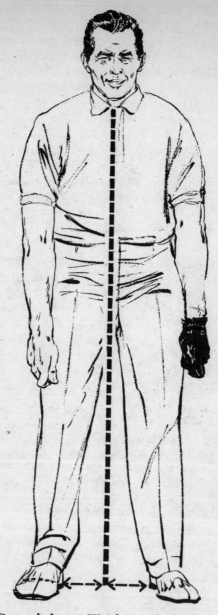

Center balance: Weight evenly divided.

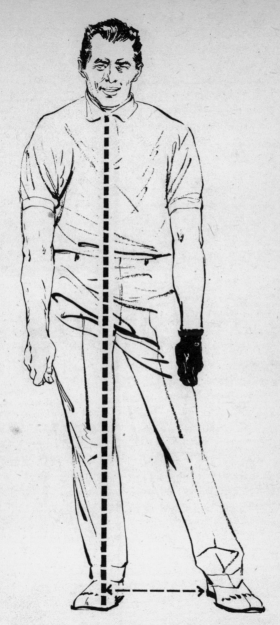

Shift to the right: Weight is on the right foot.

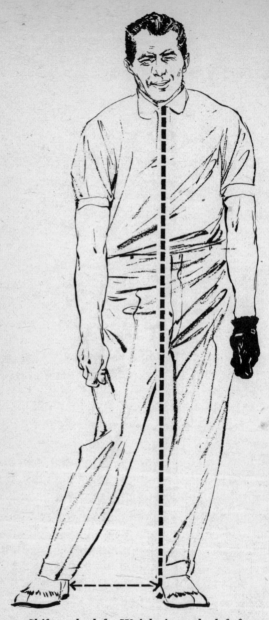

Shift to the left: Weight is on the left foot.

Adjusting your stance

It's a common statement for golfers to say, "Move the ball forward or back." Of course, the rules of golf do not permit you to move your ball around at your convenience, so all references to moving your ball positions mean you must move your foot positions to bring about the desired relation to the ball. Foot positions change quite radically. For a square stance, when using the woods, your feet will be spread about shoulder width apart, when measured from the inner edges of your shoes. From this base starting point your feet gradually move from a square to the open stance. At each change your feet move closer together until your heels are only a few inches apart.

The teed position of the ball on the drive is placed an inch or two off your left heel. Playing a five-iron, your ball will be on a line that is now centered between your heel positions because your feet have moved somewhat closer together; into an open stance. The ball position has actually not moved back very much from the drive position off the left heel. Your hands have drawn in a little to accommodate the shorter club length.

For all clubs longer than the five-iron play the ball forward of the center positions and all clubs shorter than the five-iron play back of the center position, up to a line a little forward of your right toe. This entire range of ball positions from front to back probably will not exceed four inches. If the ball is moved back, impact will be made on the downswing segment of the arc. If it is moved forward it will be on the upward segment.

Make it a habit to check these three positions—ball, hands and feet—before every shot. When you know they are right, your mind is free to think of just how you want to hit the ball.

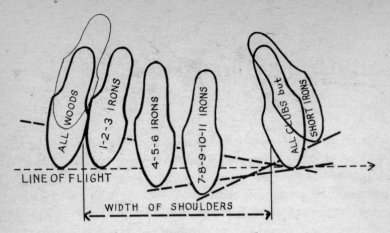

LINE OF FLIGHT

ALL WOODS

1-2-3 IRONS

4-5-6 IRONS

7-8-9-10-11 IRONS

ALL CLUBS but

SHORT IRONS

WIDTH OF SHOULDERS

Stances in relation to one another.

Foot, ball and hand position for the woods and long irons.

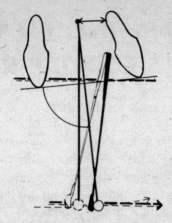

For the four-, five- and six-irons, the stance has opened slightly, the ball is on a line between your heels and the hands have moved in closer.

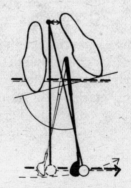

For the seven, eight, nine and wedges, the stance has opened more, causing the ball to be played toward the right foot. Again the hands have moved closer to the body.

Chapter 4

ARC AND PLANE: VITAL CONCEPTS TO YOUR GAME

The arc of your swing is the loop or invisible line made in the air by your swinging clubhead. Your arc has a shape that has many variations. The long full arc is made with your woods and long irons; the medium with the middle and short irons and finally, the very short arc with the pitch shots, chip shots and putts. In the first few feet of the swing your arc may follow the ground or pick up abruptly. These first few feet determine whether the clubhead will come into the ball on the downswing, the upswing or on the level. Adjustment in stance will help bring about this change. For example you play the woods off the left foot so that you hit them on the upswing. On the short irons you play the ball back, causing the club to hit the ball on the downswing. Shifting your center of balance forward onto your left foot, or back onto your right foot, moves the low point of your arc forward and back also.

The arc your clubhead makes influences the flight of your ball, dictating whether it flies high or low, and to some extent the amount of backspin you can apply. A common fault on short shots is to shorten your backswing arc too much by not turning your shoulders which then necessitates an exaggerated punching hand action to generate sufficient power. This invariably leads to poor distance control.

Determining the low point
of the arc

To determine the low point of the arc of your swing, take a number of practice swings on the same spot, then carefully note where you start taking the divot. This will show you where your clubhead makes contact with the turf. This is also the lowest point of your arc. Do this in several different spots with different length clubs to determine the variance with each type of club. Remember where your feet are placed in relation to that spot so you will know what correction should be made. If it is too far back you may have too much weight on your right foot and if too far forward you have too much weight on your left foot. As we said before, the center of balance changes the axis of the arc from front to back. When you have developed a fine control over your swing, you can alter this arc at will to meet the needs of the shot you choose to produce, whether it be high or low.

The lengthening or shortening of your arc by just a few inches makes a difference in the distance you hit the ball. Make sure you swing back far enough. I didn't say overswing. In the chapter dealing with the backswing you'll know what I mean.

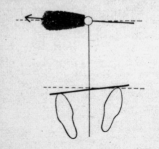

Set your body position and weight so that you will take turf at the correct spot.

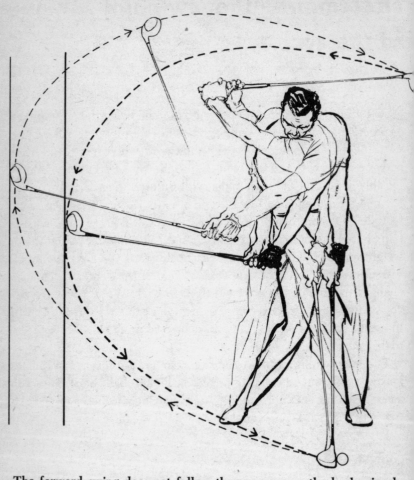

The forward swing does not follow the same arc as the backswing because your hips shift forward and your right elbow drops into your right side.

Plane

Visualize the air space enclosed within the arc of your swing as a solid, like a pie plate with your head sticking through it. This is the plane of your swing. This visualization of the pie plate makes the plane distinctly different from the arc, but of course the two are inseparable. Your plane may be set square to the line or turned sideways to an inside-out position or an outside-in position. The positions of your feet and shoulders determine the direction of the plane of your swing, whether it is inside out or outside in. Whether your plane is upright, flat or in between on the full shots will largely be dictated by your build. A short stocky player will have a flatter plane than a tall slim golfer who will swing more upright.

Inside-out plane

The plane made by the swinging clubhead starts inside the line and is continued out over the line an inch or two *after* it contacts the ball. (It ends up, as all swings must, inside the line as the club is drawn to the body at the end of the backswing.)

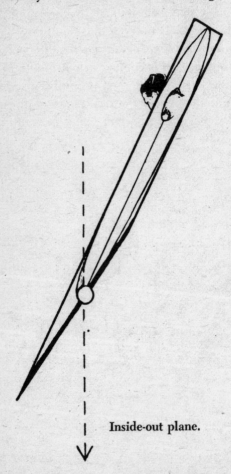

Inside-out plane.

Outside-in plane

The plane made by the swinging clubhead starts at the line but drifts out early in the backswing and is coming from outside in *before* contact with the ball. This plane is generally used for the short irons.

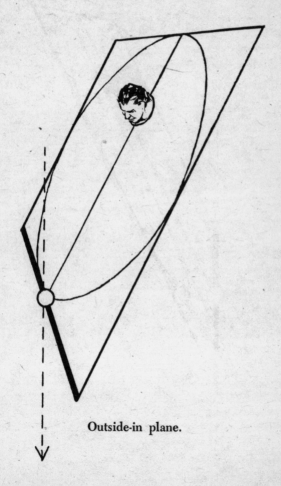

Outside-in plane.

Square plane

The plane begins and swings back along the line, goes inside the line, returns square to the ball and then on to the natural follow-through. This should be your plane for the woods and long irons.

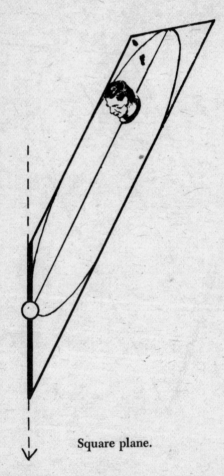

Square plane.

By first altering my stance properly, I will alter my plane to start my backswing outside to cause a slice or inside to produce a hook. This is a part of the game that should and can be understood by all golfers so that you may understand what has happened when your shots get away from you. Only when you have *mastered* the control of your plane, in other words learned how to hit a straight ball, should you even think about learning the variations (inside out or outside in). When you know you're ready to learn the variations, develop them on the practice tee first.

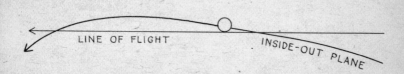

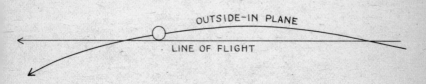

The planes in relation to the line of flight.

Part II:

Producing the Swing

Chapter 5

HANDS AND THE GRIP

Gripping your club properly is vitally important. You've probably heard that said a million times. But like a lot of oft repeated statements it's true. Think of it this way: the only contact between your body and the club is through your hands. Consequently, the way you place your hands on the club will have a lot to do with how the clubhead meets the ball.

In order to grip correctly, keep in mind that *both* your hands should work equally together. This means neither the right nor the left hand should overwhelm the other.

Left-hand grip

Your club rests on the second joint of your index finger and against the heel of your hand above the base of your little finger. When your fingers are closed your club is pressed up against the heavy pad of the heel of your hand. Hold firmly with the fingers of your left hand, but not so tight as to create tension in the cords of your wrist. Your first two knuckles are showing; your thumb is over to the right, drawn up and held against the shaft. Your right hand will press your thumb against the shaft. Study the illustrations carefully to ensure complete understanding. This is how *your* left hand should grip the club.

A strong left-hand grip is accomplished by turning your left hand to the right so that three knuckles are showing. This strong grip will encourage a hook. The reverse is true for a weak left-handed grip. Turn your hand to the left so that only one knuckle is showing. A slice or a fade will result.

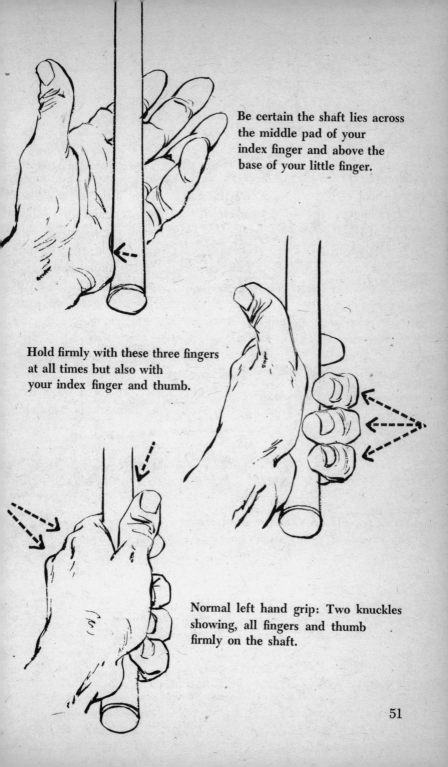

Be certain the shaft lies across the middle pad of your index finger and above the base of your little finger.

Hold firmly with these three fingers at all times but also with your index finger and thumb.

Normal left hand grip: Two knuckles showing, all fingers and thumb firmly on the shaft.

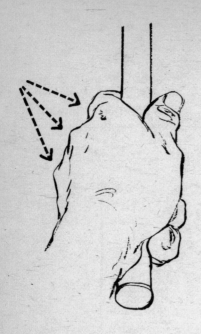

Strong grip: Hand turned to the right—three knuckles showing.

Weak grip: Hand turned to the left— one knuckle showing, thumb on top.

Right-hand grip

The shaft lies at the base of your fingers. Your thumb, forefinger and middle finger grip firmly enough to lock your club in a three-point contact so that it will not move around. In one of the drawings you'll notice the thumb has been lifted to show more clearly the action of the index finger at impact. The thumb helps hold your club firmly in place. At impact the index finger of your right hand exerts great forward pressure against the shaft and your hand and forearm exert the strength of the hitting force that you want to use. At impact both hands should be acting as one unit.

For the strong right-hand grip, the right hand is turned to the right, or under the club, so that only one knuckle is showing. Again the strong grip contributes to a hook. Conversely, the weak grip is attained by turning your right hand to the left so that two or three knuckles show. The weak right-hand grip tends to produce a fade or a slice. The danger in the weak and strong grips lies in the fact that a very slight turn in the position of one or both of your hands can make a great difference in the flight direction of the ball. Consequently, for anyone who has not yet learned how to hit a straight ball, they can prove to be disastrous to your game. Remember what we said in the introduction about a little learning being dangerous. Understand how to hit a straight ball and be able to do it consistently before you fool around with the refinements.

As you've probably noticed, we haven't discussed where you should place the little finger of your right hand. There are three acceptable methods: the overlapping or Vardon grip, the interlocking grip and the baseball or five-finger-grip. The Vardon grip, by far the most popular today, is accomplished by placing the little finger of the right hand over the forefinger of the left hand. Some years ago I changed from the interlocking to the Vardon for comfort. The interlocking grip is simply the intertwining of the index finger of the left hand with the little finger of the right. Players with small hands may find this useful. For the baseball grip, lay all your fingers on the club. Some of our finest pros find this grip helpful, e.g., Art Wall, Bob Rosburg. It is especially recommended to those with weak hands. Keep comfort in mind when you pick the one you want to use.

Finally we come to the question of what is a firm grip. This is the best explanation I can give you. Your grip should be firm enough so that (1) you don't lose the club at the top of the backswing, and (2) you can bring the clubhead into solid contact with the ball at impact. In other words a grip firm enough to maintain the same position on the club throughout the swing. Keep in mind that you'll be hitting with your hands, making it essential that your hands have remained in position.

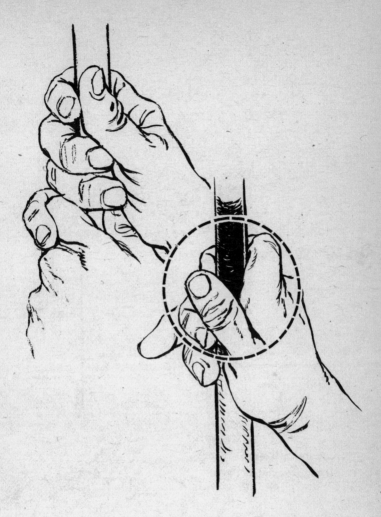

Lock your club between your thumb, index and middle finger.

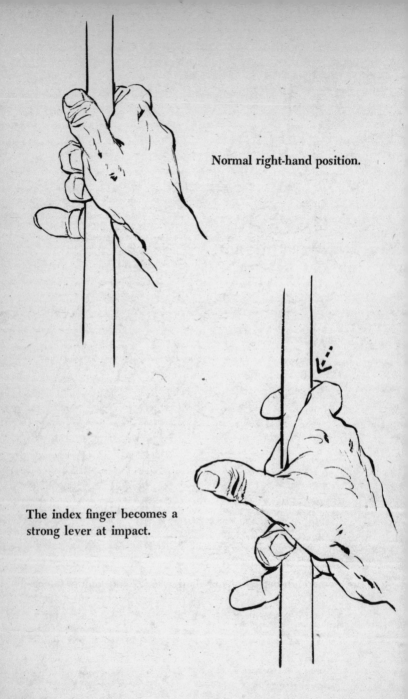

Normal right-hand position.

The index finger becomes a
strong lever at impact.

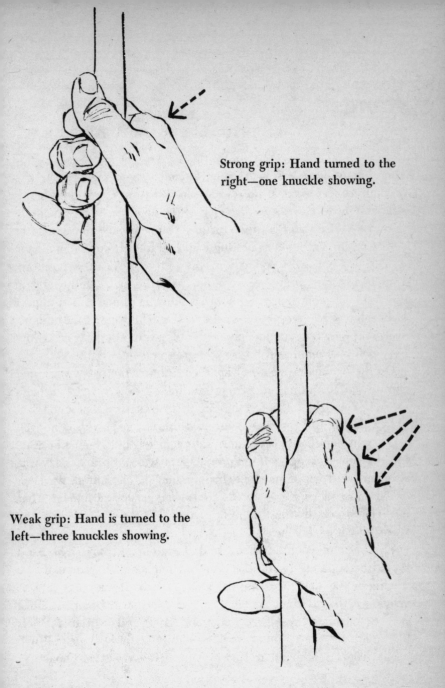

Strong grip: Hand turned to the right—one knuckle showing.

Weak grip: Hand is turned to the left—three knuckles showing.

Hands

Your hands have a subconscious tendency to come back to the normal grip positions at impact. When you turn one or both hands deliberately to a weak or strong position at address, they will try to move back to normal, thus turning your clubface to an open or closed position at impact, causing your ball to drift off line in a hook or a slice. This is why you may *choose* to use one of these positions. Your hands must bring your clubface into the ball exactly right in direction, loft and timing. Both hands function as one unit at impact but each had a job to perform prior to this. This doesn't mean, however, that they function independently of one another, but each does have points of emphasis.

On the backswing your left hand contributes the major work and control and continues its strong controlling power right through impact. Your right hand comes in with authority at about waist height on the full forward swing and exerts the power at impact, Your right hand must never dominate your left but it must be used for the power supply. If either hand is weak, tired or lazy the stronger hand will dominate. This must not be permitted. An error or loosening of your grip on the backswing reflects at impact. Your left hand especially must be in firm control at the top of your backswing to withstand the pull of the club.

The back of your left hand and the palm of your right hand should be squarely facing the target at impact with your clubface square to the line for a normal straight ball. If they are late in arriving at this desired position your clubface will be open and a slice or push will result. Should your hands roll over to the left before impact, your clubface will be closed and a hook or pull will result. Your right hand rolls over your left only after impact. If your clubhead is ahead of your hands the loft of the clubface has been increased and a scooping action occurs. Keep your wrists straight at address and at impact. If your left hand or arm weakens so that your right hand dominates there is trouble. The error is not too much right hand but not enough control in the left. It is impossible to hit too hard with your right hand if both hands bring the clubface in square to the line of flight at impact.

Your sensitivity to this very fast hand action will determine the degree of success you have in controlling the action of your ball. This is the distinguishing difference between the good and the not so good golfers. One of the greatest handicaps women have in this game is that they haven't the physical strength to permit them to manipulate their hands as freely as a fairly strong man. The lady professionals recognize this.

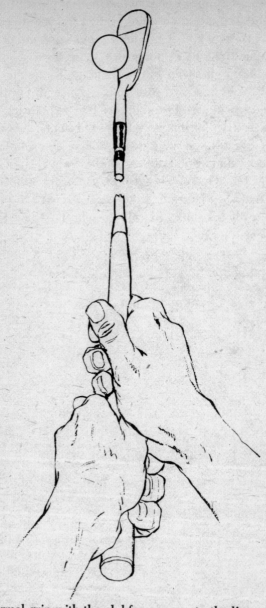

Normal grip with the clubface square to the line.

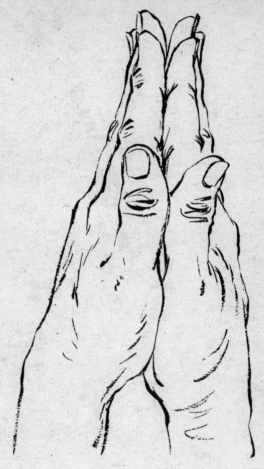

Both wrists can work smoothly together when your hands are in this position.

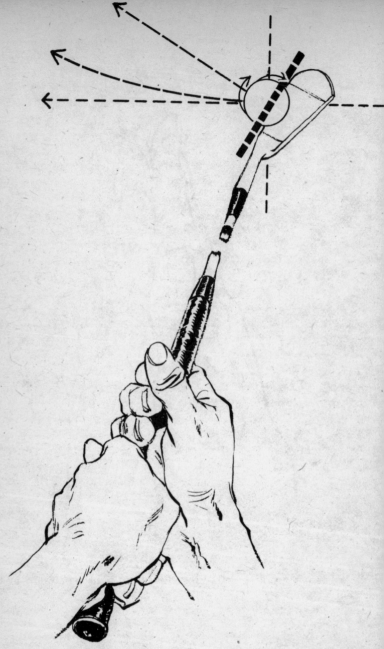

Lazy hand action has caused the club to come into the ball with the face open. Slice or push results.

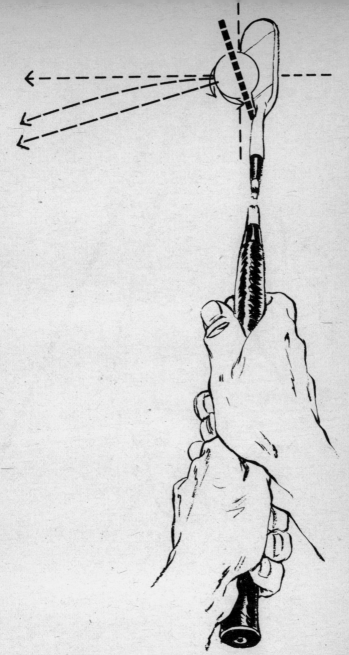

Hands have rolled over before impact, closing the clubface and the resulting hook or pull.

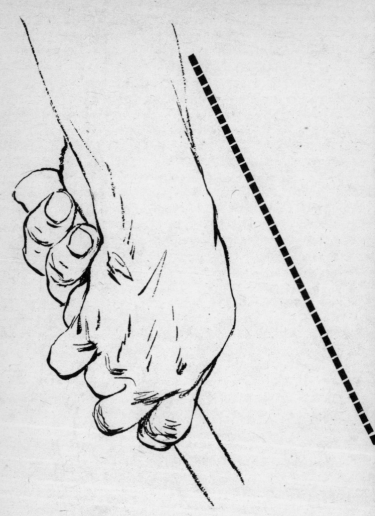

Keep your wrists straight at address and impact.

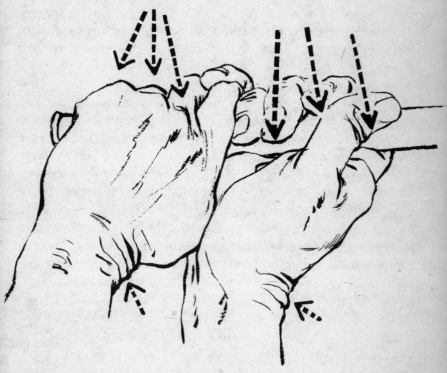

Front view at the top of your backswing—wrists fully cocked, left hand firmly in control, right hand correctly gripped and positioned.

The waggle

The waggle, which is principally hand action, gives you the feeling of your club in your hands. While in this waggling motion you are probing for a good sense of positioning and balance, but primarily the action provides a miniature warm-up for the character or kind of shot you wish to produce. It may be slow and smooth, fast and crisp or anywhere in between. It's all dictated by the shot you need to make. The way you waggle is a very personal thing, but however you choose to do it, standardize your action so that you repeat it each time you step up to the ball. I have been doing it the same way for thirty years. I approach the ball, bring my feet together, set my club in proper position, spread my feet for the shot I mean to make, waggle my club twice, set it behind the ball for a momentary pause, forward press and then glide into my backswing. After I start my first action toward the ball I am in motion, except for the slight pause before the backswing starts, until I have completed my follow-through. Because it has become an ingrained habit I have only to think of what I want to do with my ball. This simplifies my procedure. This is the reason why folks say I waste no time when I step up to the ball. By then I know what I mean to do and I don't fuss around doing it.

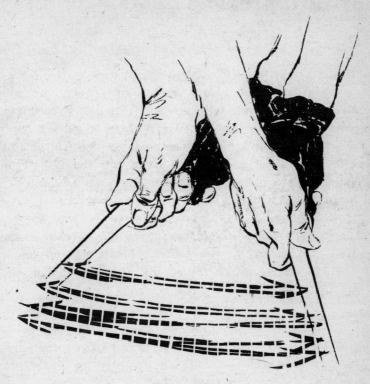

The waggle.

Forward press

The forward press is not affectation or idle gesture. It is done by easing your right knee an inch or two toward your left knee, which causes your hips to turn a bit to the left. This allows your forward press movement to be smooth and easy, from which you can rebound into the backswing in one continuous motion. This, with the shoulder turn, is the start of your backswing and is frequently called the one-piece swing. Your hands may press a little forward but this is the result of your knee action, not a conscious act in itself.

The value of the forward press lies in starting your body into motion gently. Without it your body is on dead center, standing still, and your backswing is more likely to start with an impulsive jerk, due to tenseness, which will upset your smooth rhythm.

Forward press.

Chapter 6

THE DEPENDABLE BACKSWING

The proper backswing is the most crucial part of the repeating swing. The very first move of the backswing—the first few inches—determines everything which will come later. If something is wrong in the beginning some compensation will have to be made to bring about correct contact at impact. (In most cases this leads to further disaster.)

The term "one-piece swing" has been so abused and misinterpreted that I hesitate to use it—but here it is: If you can visualize yourself, at address, as cast in solid concrete from the hips up, with movement only in your wrists and neck, it might help you to understand how important this starting spot is. Although concrete would be rigid you must not feel rigid or tense.

As we said before, the rebound action of the forward press is the initiator of your backswing. Now start back by turning your shoulders and everything else will move smoothly and slowly. This will help prevent jerking, lifting and swaying. It's worth repeating. *Turn with your shoulders*. Swing back as far as you comfortably can and if you have kept undue tension out of your arms, your wrists will cock or break naturally. You would have to act deliberately to stop them from cocking.

Throughout the entire swing your left arm should remain comfortably straight and in complete and constant control. Your right hand retains a firm but inactive grip. When fully turned you will be looking at your ball over your left shoulder. Your left foot has rolled onto its inner edge and your left knee will be bent toward your right foot. The left heel remains on the ground or it may lift off slightly, never very much. Pressure should be felt on the inner edges of both feet.

The backswing should be smooth and easy as all it is doing is pulling the left side muscles taut, like pulling back a bowstring. A fast backswing doesn't contribute any extra power but it will upset control. The fallacy that you have to swing hard and fast is one that everyone should get over now. It is impossible to hit the ball well consistently if you're swinging too fast.

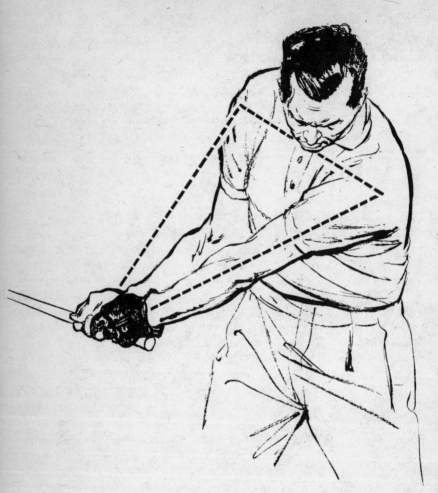

Torso, shoulders and hands turn back together as though there were no separate movement possible in any part, thus the term "one-piece swing." Turn without tension in any part.

Let your shoulders swing your hands back.

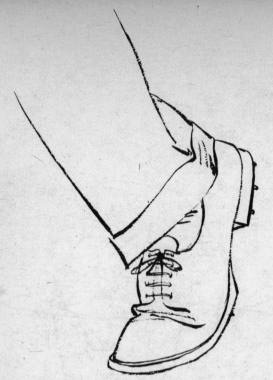

Incorrect: Never be up on your toes.

Correct: Left foot rolls on its inner edge.

The backswing pulls the left side muscles taut, like pulling back a bow-string.

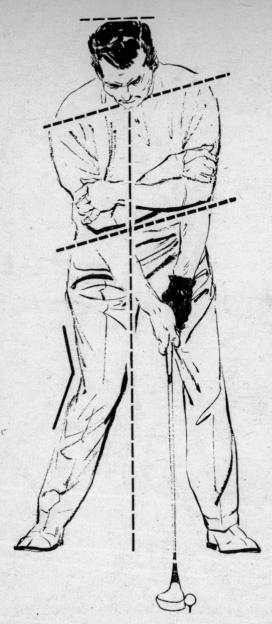

Backswing sequence: Begin with your weight a little heavier on your right foot—ball about two inches back of your left heel. Right knee bent left a little—all parts firm but relaxed.

Your shoulders start to swing your hands back. A smooth one-piece take-away at this point is all important. Your hips will follow naturally.

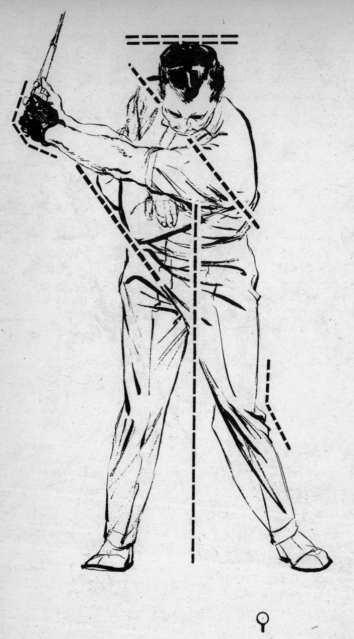

This is as far back as you can go on the backswing without a full shoulder turn.

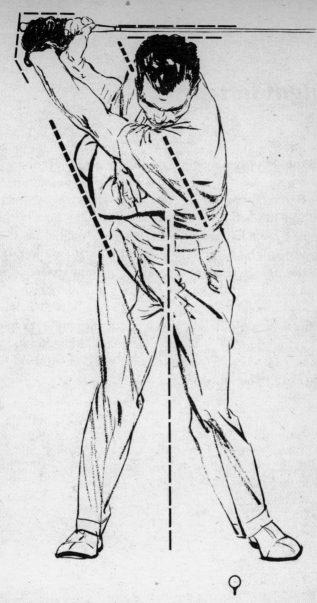

The full shoulder turn—wrists are cocked and left heel may be slightly off the ground. Now go back over the last four illustrations. Fold your arms as illustrated and perform the same full turn as though you had a club in your hands. This is what your shoulders do when you do have a club. Let your shoulders swing your hands back.

Straight left arm

The necessity of maintaining a straight left arm is a concept I want to impress upon you. At address your left arm is easily held comfortably straight, establishing the exact distance between your shoulder and the ball. This distance must be the same at impact. If, at impact, your left arm is bent or your shoulder has raised or lowered, you will hit behind the ball or top it. If your left shoulder glides to the right as a result of swaying or turns too far around to the left on your forward swing, a fade or a pull may occur.

Without a straight left arm, the long full arc, which is instrumental in producing distance, is just about impossible. A bent left arm will permit your shaft to drop far below the horizontal at the top of your backswing, making a smooth start on the forward swing very difficult. As you can see, there is a reason for everything in the correct golf swing.

At address your left arm is held comfortably straight, establishing the exact distance between your shoulder and the ball. This distance must be the same at impact.

Right elbow "under" the club shaft brings your elbow comfortably into your side aiding the straight shot.

Right elbow "flying" contributes to a slice by encouraging an outside-in plane.

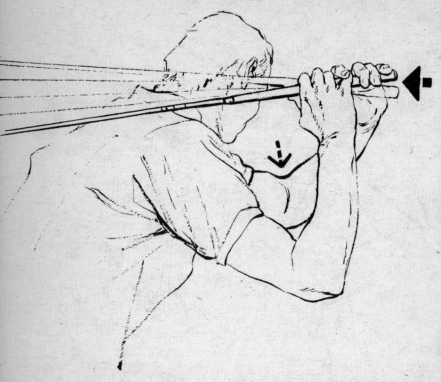

A bent left arm will permit your shaft to drop far below the horizontal, making a smooth start on the forward swing very difficult.

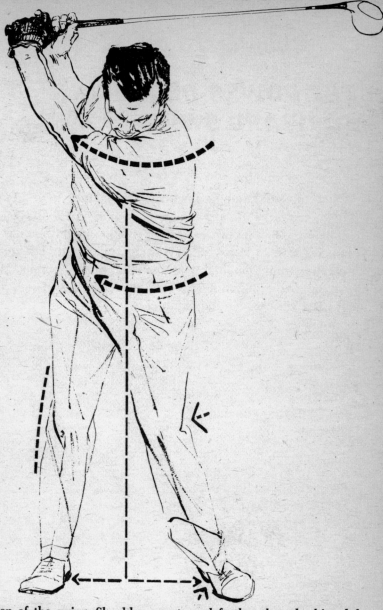

The top of the swing. Shoulders are turned further than the hips, left arm is straight, wrists are fully cocked. Club is almost horizontal in closed position. Right knee is slightly flexed; left knee is bent to the right. Left foot has rolled onto its inner edge. When you are in this ideal position at the top of the backswing, you are "set" to start your forward swing.

Chapter 7

THE POWER-PRODUCING FORWARD SWING

As your forward swing or downswing starts, your left side muscles start to contract in proper sequence. They start contracting gently just before your backswing has been completed which is the reason for being able to stop your backswing under control. This is like gently applying your brakes so that you can glide smoothly into your forward swing without a jerk. (Practice this in slow motion and study each part in the sequence.)

Chain action

First your left heel goes down to the ground which causes your left knee to straighten some. Your hips slide laterally around and toward the left as your leg and hip muscles pull. Your left leg now becomes the strong anchor point of resistance, around or against which the rest of the action takes place. The chain action now pulls your shoulders around and your left shoulder and back muscles start slowly pulling your left arm down. The strong muscles of your right chest are pulling your right arm down. Your shoulders and hands are moving as a unit just as they did on the backswing. Let your shoulders lead your hands down. Your forward swing starts smoothly and slowly and as your powerful shoulder and back muscles come into full play the entire action picks up momentum.

At the point where your left arm has pulled your hands down to about waist height, which is the start of the hitting zone, your right elbow should be brushing lightly into your right side. Your right elbow is still bent at almost a right angle and your wrists are still in a fully cocked position. At this point your weight is pretty evenly balanced on both feet. Your right knee is pulling in toward the ball, forcing your weight against your left leg which is straightening and providing the necessary resistance for hitting power. The straightening of your left knee at this point pushes your body up from the "sitting down" position. Your left shoulder goes up and your right shoulder comes in under, square to the intended line of flight. Your shoulders turn fast enough to bring them square to the line in good timing and you hit with your hands. It is an easy mistake to turn your shoulders too fast at this point, as if you were hitting with your shoulders, thus losing the feeling of control in your hands.

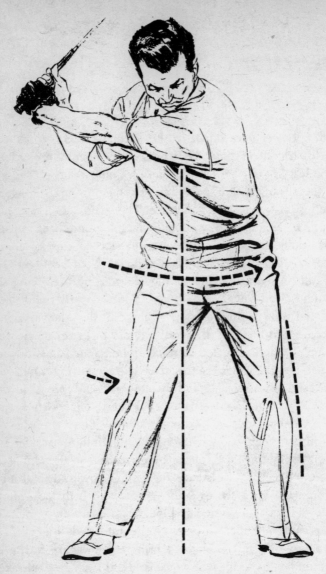

Forward-swing sequence: The hips have shifted laterally and turned. Push is against the left leg. Balance is centered.

Shoulders are turning, pulling the arms down. Right elbow has dropped into the side. Wrists are fully cocked as they approach the hitting zone.

The hips have shifted fully and turned out of the way of the hands. Right shoulder has come in under, square to the line. Right forearm has straightened, wrists have released, lashing the clubhead into the ball. The upper body weight has remained behind the ball.

The explosive blast-off

Now comes the explosive blast-off. The unwinding body pivot continues smoothly. Your right elbow straightens forcefully, and because of the great speed your clubhead is already traveling, your cocked wrists will be forced to release your hands. The speed you choose to use is determined by you beforehand. The faster your clubhead speed the farther your ball should go if contacted solidly. Your right side has taken positive action. Your left hip has turned past the line a little as it must be in the lead and out of the way of your hands. After impact your body weight moves onto and beyond your left foot in a continuous motion to a complete follow-through, which causes you to roll onto the outer edge of your left foot.

Study the sequence action illustrations carefully and note the action that takes place between the top of the backswing and the first illustration of the forward swing. This is a very critical stage. Note how much my hips have turned and shifted laterally and how little my shoulders have turned. The second illustration shows how my right elbow has dropped into my side because my shoulders have come around that much. Although each of these movements do take place as I have described them they follow each other so rapidly that it feels like everything is moving in "one piece." You shouldn't be conscious of any separate actions.

Wrists uncocking too soon causes a great loss of hitting power and contributes to an outside-in plane.

Wrists releasing after your hands have reached the hitting zone, contributing to a greater hitting force. From this point to impact is the hitting zone.

Your hands may or may not roll over quickly following impact; mine do. There should be no roll over before impact. Your hands come into the ball square.

SWING EASY, HIT HARD

Probably the heart of the action which makes my swing look easy, and which brings about the title of this book, *Swing Easy, Hit Hard,* lies in this chapter. I never feel that I am in danger of being too fast on my backswing simply because my shoulders just won't start too fast. As my hands reach the hitting zone I can increase their speed to anything I choose within my capabilities. So here you have the secret. *Turn with your shoulders, hit with your hands.*

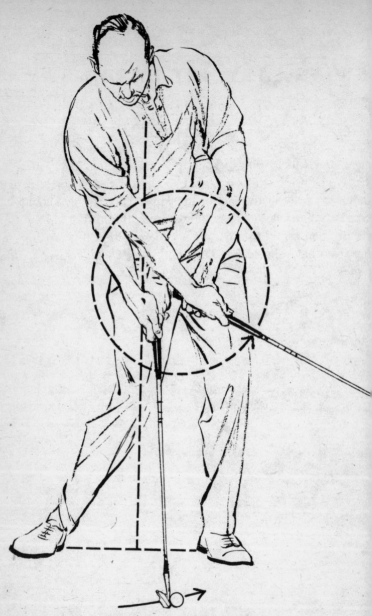

Scooping hand action: The hands are bringing the clubhead into the ball at impact ahead of the hands. This generally occurs as a result of the body falling back. Clubhead speed is badly dissipated as a consequence.

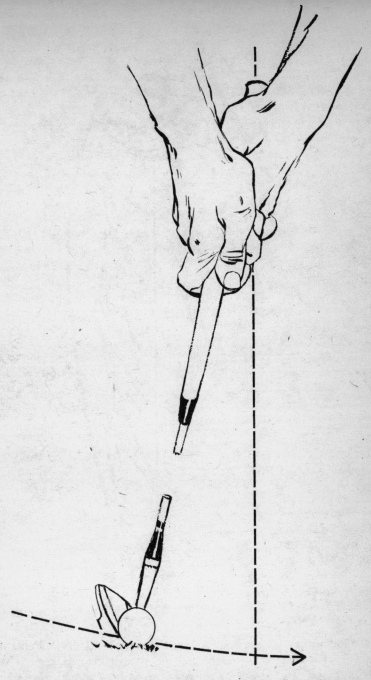

Correct action: Hands are leading the clubhead into impact.

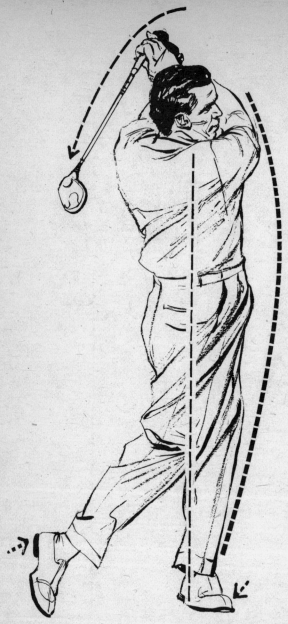

In the follow-through, the body weight has moved past the ball onto the left foot. The body has straightened up, though the left knee is still slightly flexed. The enormous clubhead speed is permitted to continue until its own inertia stops it.

Chapter 8

HOW THE WEIGHT SHIFTS

Lateral movement

The question of whether your body weight shifts from side to side has been discussed for years and the consensus of opinion is that it does. However, the mechanics and the reasons for the shift should be clearly understood.

You start at the address by having your weight evenly balanced between both feet and distributed on the balls and the heels of your feet. Your shoulders start your backswing and as your hands reach about waist height a feeling of push goes over to your right leg; a feeling that causes you to believe that your weight has shifted onto your right leg. Your right knee should remain slightly flexed. *There is little, if any, lateral movement.* Because your hips have now turned on your backswing your left foot must roll onto the inner edge of the ball of your foot. Your heel should leave the ground very little. Make sure you don't go up on your toes at this point. Remember it robs you of precious balance. Your left foot must be in a position to carry the weight that is on your left side at the top of your backswing. Your left knee bends sideways, toward the right, allowing your hips to turn to the right. This sideway bend of your left knee is vitally important. If your knee only dips down and forward, as is frequently done, there is no turning action to your hips and very little on your shoulders. Consequently your left shoulder drops down, dangerously shortening the distance between your left shoulder and the ball. If you don't raise up in time, you're going to hit behind the ball. If you raise up too quickly you'll top it. The action becomes an up and down pumping motion instead of a smooth unwinding turn, causing the loss of considerable hitting power.

From the feeling of pausing at the top of your swing, which indictates that you are in perfect balance and control, the action reverses itself on the downswing. Your hips turn and move laterally to the left which creates a strong push against your left leg. Your upper body weight has remained behind the ball, which keeps you in balance, and your right shoulder moves down and under, square to the line of flight. Your entire upper body weight is moving into the ball at impact but must not move ahead of the ball until after impact. That is what your entire structure must be doing at impact. All in one piece, perfectly coordinated and timed.

At impact: Your hips have shifted ahead of the center balance line. Your upper body remains in balance behind the ball. Thus your entire weight is moving into the ball at impact.

Hitting high or low

"Heavy on the left foot" or "heavy on the right foot" is a good way to remember how to deliberately shift your weight for a purpose. If you want your ball to stay low put your weight forward on your left foot at address and keep it there at impact. Reverse this procedure onto your right foot if you want your ball to go high.

Low ball: Weight is shifted to the left foot at address and remains there throughout the swing.

Low ball: Play your ball a bit back of normal. The axis has tilted forward so the clubhead continues its downward arc into the turf after impact.

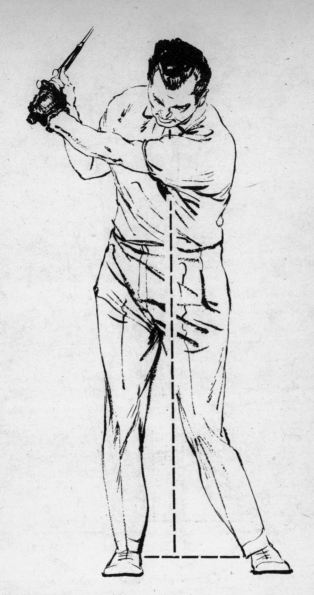

High ball: Body weight is shifted onto right foot at address and remains there through impact.

High ball: Play the ball forward. The axis of your arc has tilted back. The club meets the ball at the point of your arc where your clubhead is moving horizontally and you pick the ball off clean and follow-through completely.

Timing

The best way I can think of to explain timing is to say, "Timing is being at the right place at the right time." In other words your arms, hands, shoulders, hips, etc., will be at the places they should be in the swing at the proper time. Good timing is achieved by coordinating all the independent parts of your swing into one smooth over-all swing. The sooner you learn to coordinate these parts the sooner you'll play golf well.

Have you ever wondered why a great pro will have a few bad months or perhaps even a bad year? More times than not it's because some deviation or hitch has crept into his swing, throwing his timing off. It may take him a while to find it, but when he does he'll be back in there winning the money. When you've developed a pretty good swing keep this in mind. If something goes wrong, take some time out and practice. That's what I do. If after practicing you still can't find the hitch, take a lesson from your local pro. It can save you a lot of time and golf enjoyment.

Proper timing: All parts are moving in perfect coordination and balance at impact.

Part III:

Now Let's Hit
Some Shots

Chapter 9

THINK AND SAVE STROKES

Playing the course

You and I would not play any course in the same way, because our abilities and techniques are not the same. And I don't mean mine are better than yours, just different. You must play the course within your capabilities. To do this, it is essential to recognize your strengths and weaknesses. If your strength is in your short game, try to improve your long game by devoting most of your practice time to it. The same holds true for the strong long game.

When you come to a hole, plan your strategy before you tee up. It's really quite simple, yet for some unknown reason most weekend golfers don't do it. An example of how it helped me occurred at the '63 Open at The Country Club in Brookline, Massachusetts, on the 17th hole. The hole, a slight dogleg to the left, measures about 380 yards. There is a large tree alongside the right-hand portion of the green which blocks that side of the green. Three days out of five (the four days of regular play ended in a tie, necessitating the extra day for the play-off) the pin was tucked in back of this overhanging tree. A long straight drive would place the ball on the right-hand side of the fairway with the tree between the player and the pin. Four out of the five rounds I drove with a one-iron, the other time with a three-wood, ending up a little short on the left side. This left me with an eight-iron to the green, instead of a nine-iron or wedge if I had used a driver, but I had a straight shot to the pin with no interference from the tree. I birdied this hole three out of five times and this contributed greatly to my winning the tournament. Would you have thought ahead, and played the hole that way? You'll find yourself saving many strokes per round if you use your common sense and plan ahead.

111

Trouble shots

At one time or another every golfer finds himself off the fairway, faced with a difficult shot. Sometimes you can't avoid having to accept the loss of a stroke or two to get back into play. If that's the story, accept it and consider yourself lucky it wasn't worse. What can make it worse is to try to get back into play by means of a miraculous shot, often leading to three or four extra strokes. This rarely happens to a smart golfer. He knows his game and what he can and cannot do.

On the other hand, situations that often look like trouble are really not trouble at all. A flat lie in the rough isn't any different from a flat lie in the fairway. Don't get the jitters just because it's the rough. Should conditions be such that you cannot swing or stand normally, then you must make the necessary adjustments. Take the most comfortable stance you can find, grip down on the shaft if necessary, swing back with deliberate control and *stroke* the ball out. Don't tighten up and pound at the ball viciously. The main thing to remember on these shots is to relax and stroke the ball. In "playing safe" to get out of trouble, you must still use your head to avoid going from one trap to another or coming out of the woods and crossing to the woods on the other side. Hit just hard enough to get the ball back into play.

Here are two dependable rules to follow when you're in a difficult situation: (1) Decide whether the penalty is worth taking, especially within the limits of your shot-producing capabilities. (2) If you decide to play the shot, use your ingenuity. For example, if you have to play a left-handed shot away from a tree, fence, etc., your putter might be just the club to turn the trick.

Not long ago, I had an interesting dilemma. I hit a shot which landed green high but off to one side, about six inches from an out-of-bounds stone wall. Because I couldn't get a club between the ball and the wall, I played my shot into the wall and bounced it onto the green. Admittedly they're usually not that dramatic but a more extensive use of your imagination might solve some of those troublesome situations.

Chapter 10
EVERYDAY SHOTS

Driving

I'm sure you've all heard the cliché, "Drive for show, putt for dough." Nothing could be further from the truth. No player can win the U.S. Open or any other major tournament who can't keep his drives in play. This is largely what separates the winners from the losers.

When I am getting off the tee my first concern is to stay on the fairway. Unless of course the character of the hole demands that I place my tee shot to the right or left side to facilitate an easier second shot. This should be your first consideration too. Be on the fairway. The same mechanics apply to driving as to any other shot. Because you are playing the shot off your left heel you will contact the ball either on the upswing or as the club is running parallel to the ground. This is as it should be. On your drives you do not want backspin nor do you want to take turf, you want the ball to fly in the air for as long as possible and then to roll as far as possible. Again, let your primary consideration be to place the ball on the fairway.

Consistency of form is a necessity. My advice is: Find what is good form for you and then repeat it consistently until it is a normal pattern or habit. Like a guy who puts his left shoe on first every morning. Perhaps this is why I look as though I am playing fast once I approach the ball.

Incorrect: Hitting down on the ball creates backspin causing the ball to climb and drop sharply with little roll.

Correct: Ball hit squarely on the back or on the upswing, carries far, getting maximum roll.

Fairway woods

As the pros play the game today there are not many occasions to use a wood off the fairway. They are getting distances that make any hole other than the longest par fours and fives reachable with an iron for the second shot. However, this is not true for the week-end players. For them the three-, four- and five-woods are indispensable. Here's how to play them: If your ball is sitting up on the grass nicely, play it off your left heel or much the same as you would from the tee. Sweep it off clean without taking any turf. If it is nestled down tight, play your ball back an inch or two and hit down and through it as you would with a long iron, taking a little turf out in front of it. This shot will fade a little, so play it a bit to the left.

The fairway woods are particularly valuable in the rough. If you have a flat lie or better, very often a wood will get the ball out with greater efficiency than an iron. Probably the reason the weekend golfer depends on these clubs rather than the long irons is because with their longer shaft and bigger head they look as though they should get greater distance with less effort. Consequently the golfer swings easier and smoother with them. There is an important point here. If you could approach every club with the confidence you have with your favorite club, your swing would be more relaxed and hence capable of producing the best results. Try to approach each shot this way and see if it doesn't help.

When using a fairway wood from a tight lie, hit down on it much like an iron.

Long irons

Probably the clubs which the average golfer thinks are the hardest to play are the long irons. They're really not any harder to hit than the other clubs. Let me ask you a question. How many times in your life have you practiced them? Most of the weekend golfers I know have rarely if ever practiced the long irons. Why don't you try them out? There are many situations on the golf course where they're invaluable.

For the one-, two- and three-irons, I play a square stance with my ball placed a little back of my driving position. Be sure to take a full shoulder turn. Let the club do the work; the loft and the length of the shaft will take care of the distance. Don't press for anything extra; the secret here is smoothness. The arc of your swing should reach its lowest point a bit in front of the ball which means at impact your clubhead is swinging down. The ball has started its flight before your club actually contacts the ground. Naturally you will take turf, but less than with the short irons. The plane is more upright than with the woods but the sweeping swing is much the same except, again, for the low point of the arc.

The purpose of the long irons is to get needed distance with accuracy. Occasionally I will play a one- or two-iron from the tee of a par-four hole because control is essential and the distance I lose presents no handicap. My early golf was played on a long course where I had to learn to use the long irons. Consequently I can hit a two-iron with almost as much accuracy as I can a shorter iron. You can too, if you practice and play them.

Long iron and wood stance.

Medium irons

The medium irons (four, five and six) are used with a great deal of confidence by the average player. Probably because the first club most new golfers start with is the five-iron. A slight change of stance is used for the medium irons.

Open your stance and move your right foot a bit closer to your left. (Study the diagram to understand this more fully.) Your ball position will appear now to be about midway between your feet. Actually your ball position hasn't changed. This is what happens: Your right side moves closer to the ball when you adopt the open stance. This also moves your hands forward although they remain in the same relation to your left foot. With the open stance your backswing will now be shorter and more upright. The medium irons are excellent trouble retrievers. They will give you a great variety of loft and all the distance you can rightfully expect from bad spots.

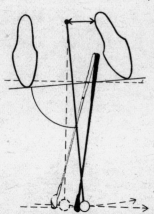

Open your stance slightly for the medium irons.

Short irons

The short irons (seven, eight, nine and wedges) are the clubs with which you should be most accurate. Because your stance has opened more and your feet are closer together, your swing is shorter and should be much better controlled. It's well worth your time and energy to learn to play these well. They can save you a lot of strokes if you can get up there for one putt after a bad second shot.

To play a full shot with any of these clubs, move your feet quite close together so there is only about ten inches between your heels. Open your stance a bit more than with your medium irons. The normal flight of the ball on a full shot will be very high, causing the ball to come down at a nearly perpendicular angle with little forward impetus.

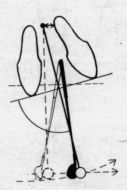

For the short irons, adjust your stance so there is only about ten inches between your heels.

Pitching and chipping

Here's a shot I used with great effectiveness in winning the '63 Open. I call it the soft-wedge pitch. It can be played with either a sand or pitching wedge. Stroke the ball so that at impact you get the club *under the ball,* lifting it into the air and down on the green softly with little forward roll. The entire action is dependent on a smooth shoulder turn. The backswing is a controlled hand action with quite a long arc to prevent jabbing or punching. The shot can only be played from a good lie. Do not play it from a tight or flat lie on the fairway or in the rough. There *must* be sufficient room under the ball for the club to get under. Play the ball forward, off your left foot. It's a useful shot to know but its success depends on practice.

On the chip shots from the fringe of the green or a little further out it is generally advisable to use a straight-faced club. Which you choose, however, should be determined by the shot. For example, if you are on the fringe above the hole (shooting downhill) you're probably better off with an eight- or nine-iron so you get as little roll as possible. Conversely, if you were below the hole (shooting uphill) a two- or three-iron might be best. Which club you use is largely personal. The important thing is to use the one which gives you confidence.

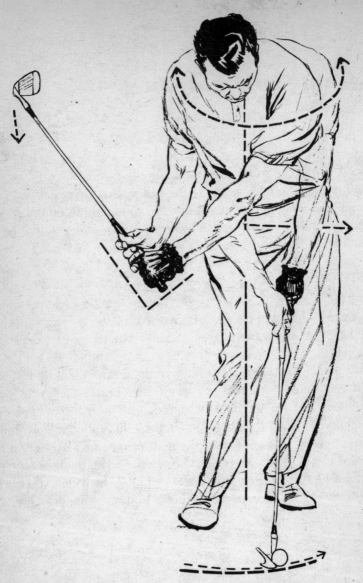

Soft wedge pitch: An important feature of this shot is that it must be
executed with a free shoulder turn, an ample backswing and controlled
sensitive hand action. The ball is lobbed softly onto the green and rolls
very little. This shot is played much like a sand shot.

For pitches from the long grass, the clubhead reaches the low point of the arc an inch or two behind the ball and is moving parallel to the ground at impact, getting under the ball and lifting it out gently. The grass between the ball and club reduces backspin, causing the ball to run farther.

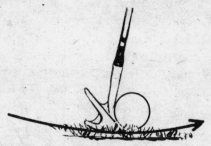

When the fairway grass is deep and soft it is ideal for the soft wedge pitch. Bring the clubhead into the ball at the low point of the arc, getting under the ball.

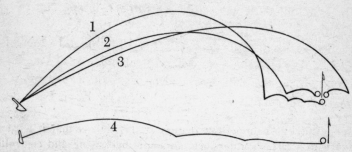

1. Soft pitch.
2. Pitch with normal backspin.

3. Pitch with extreme backspin.
4. Pitch and run.

Putting

Putting is a personal thing. How you place your feet or grip the club or swing is not all-important. What is important is that your blade is square to the line of your choosing at impact and the ball is hit solidly. This point can't be stressed enough. You have half the secret of putting if you can bring the blade into the ball solidly. The next time there's a tournament on television notice the difference in the ways the pros putt. It's very difficult to find two which are the same. They're all searching for the stroke, stance, etc., which will bring their blade into the ball squarely and solidly time after time. You should be too.

Here is the way that I've found best for me. Try it, perhaps it will work well for you. First decide the line the ball will have to take to go into the hole. Will it break left or right, or go straight? When you've decided on the line, address the ball with your feet almost touching, knees bent slightly to relieve tension. Play the ball off your left toe. Now swing the blade back slowly, close to the ground, using little wrist and shoulder motion. The forward stroke is smooth and the follow-through natural. I hold my head and body as still as I comfortably can without tension, but certainly not rigidly.

Practice is essential to good putting. Unfortunately there is no alternative. Develop the feeling that the club is part of you. Handle it, use it, stroke balls with it whenever or wherever you can so that you have confidence in it as with an old friend. If you can't get out for some reason, practice putting on a flat rug; every bit of practice helps.

My feet are close together which places my ball off the toe of my left foot. I use a fairly long stroke and follow-through with a slight shoulder action. My left firmly controls the stroke and my right hand determines the hitting power but I am not conscious of any separate actions.

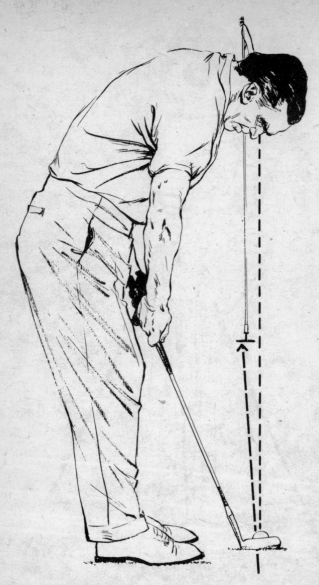

I position my ball so that my eyes are directly over it. My hands are in close. Both hands are square to the hole. I try to bring my hands and clubhead straight back and through my intended line.

Chapter 11

UNUSUAL SHOTS AND PROBLEMS

Sand shots

Probably the shot most feared by weekend golfers is the trap shot. Until you've learned the mechanics of how to play the shot, they can be very troublesome. But after you've learned how, you'll wonder at the simplicity of it all.

First let's consider the sand shot right around the green. The easiest way to be certain of getting out is to play an "explosion" shot. Open your stance about the same way you would for a short iron. Now work your feet into the sand for a solid footing. Next, shorten your grip and play the ball an inch or so inside the left heel. Open your clubface slightly and swing back breaking your wrists sharply. As you come into the ball, turn your left hip out of the way and hit two or three inches behind the ball. Keep your hands ahead of the clubhead and continue the action to a complete follow-through. A common and fatal error is to stop the club after hitting the sand. (Study the illustrations closely for a complete understanding of this shot.)

The texture of the sand will influence this shot a great deal. If the sand is hard and wet, dig deep into the sand and swing a little harder. If the sand is dry and crusty, swing a little easier. Remember, the harder the sand is to cut through the harder you have to hit. The easier it is to cut through the easier you swing.

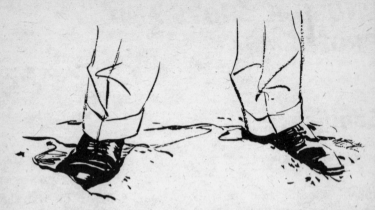

Work your feet down into the sand to avoid slipping.

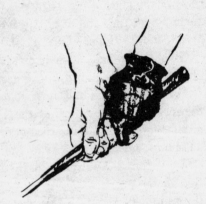

Shorten up on your grip.

Explosion shot sequence: Both knees flexed and relaxed. Weight a little more on the left foot. Clubface opened.

Shoulder turn with wrists cocking abruptly. Weight stays on left foot.

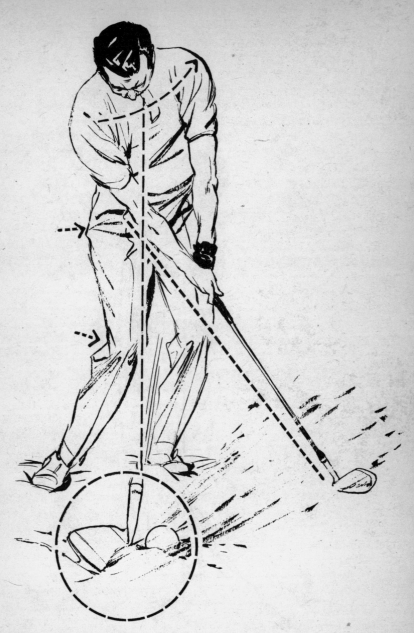

Hit down about two to three inches in back of the ball. Weight is moving forward.

Follow-through completely.

Buried trap shots

You've all seen these. It's the shot that stays in the hole it makes when landing in the trap. Don't be afraid of it; it's not hard to play. Close the face of your sand wedge and hit down hard about three to five inches behind the ball. (Using, of course, the swing and stance of the explosion shot.) Your club must dig deep to get under the ball and bump it out. The shot will come out low and roll a bit farther than the normal trap shot. Coming out of a trap along the side of the green, under normal conditions, you should expect to get within one putt range most every time. That is, once you've gained confidence in the shot. Confidence is at least 50 percent of the sand shot.

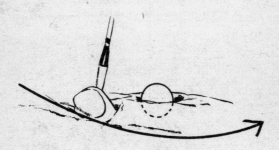

Buried or plugged ball.

Long trap shots

Almost as important as how to hit this shot is the proper selection of the club. Realize two things: First, you won't get as much distance from a club out of the trap as you would in the fairway. In other words, if you were on the fairway alongside the trap and needed a five-iron to the green, you'd need a four-iron from the sand trap. Secondly, make sure the club you've selected can clear the lip of the trap. Your primary consideration in trap shots is to get out of them.

As a general rule, don't use a wood from a trap unless your lie is perfect and the lip of the trap is low enough and far away enough to permit the ball to rise above it. Let's look now at hitting the shot. Again make sure your feet are set solidly as there is a tendency to slip in the sand. Play the ball as you would from a tight lie in the fairway. Open your stance a little and allow for a slight fade. The essential effort in the execution of this shot is to hit the ball first.

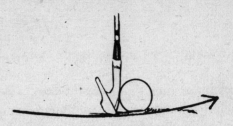

Medium iron played from the sand. Pick it almost clean from the low point of the arc.

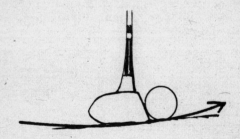

Wood played from the trap. Pick it off with as little sand as possible.

The sand wedge

The wide-soled wedge is an indispensable tool. If you don't own one, I'd advise getting one. No other club can do the same job. Another of its uses is the pitch shot from the heavy rough. Sometimes only a heavy club will dig you out. One thing you can be sure of, every pro carries a sand wedge in his bag.

Sidehill lie

A situation most every golfer will face at least once a round is the sidehill lie. Though the fairway you are playing looks perfectly level as you look down it toward the green, you may find as you arrive at your ball that you have a subtle sidehill lie of some type or variation. Perhaps it's just a slight undulation or hollow, but that's enough to change the normal relation of the position of the ball to your hands and feet. You should be aware of the changes and position yourself accordingly. Keep one thing in mind. Swing normally with a shorter backswing so that you can maintain balance. On the sidehill and uphill lies, where golfers are apt to lose some distance, many players lose all self-control and swing wildly. Try to keep a smooth and easy rhythm to your swing.

Uphill lie

This is one of the easier sidehill shots to hit. Because of the slope of the land, your right foot is lower than your left, throwing your weight onto your right foot just as though you were deliberately playing your ball high, which is precisely what you are doing. Play your ball a little forward toward your left or higher foot. Your left knee must bend at address to make your balance position comfortable. Shorten your grip and open your stance. Use a longer club than you would normally use since your ball will go higher with less distance. Aim a little to the right of your normal target line.

Uphill lie: Weight is on your lower foot. Play your ball a little forward toward your higher foot. Shorten your grip and open your stance. Use a longer club because your ball will go higher. Aim to the right of the target.

Downhill lie

This lie is apt to make you feel cramped on your backswing. Your weight is forward on your left foot (lower foot). Your right knee bends to accommodate the forced change in balance and your ball position is played back a little toward your higher foot. Again shorten your grip and open your stance. Be precise in setting the position and angle of your clubface, keep it square to the line. Your backswing will need to be abrupt because of the interfering slope. Aim your ball a little to the left.

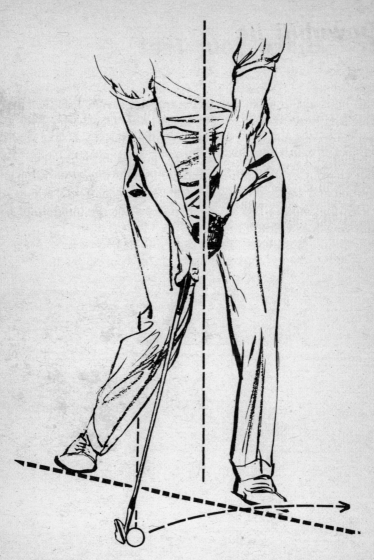

Downhill lie: Weight is on lower foot. Ball is played back toward the higher foot. Again shorten your grip and open your stance. Aim to the left of the target.

Ball above your feet

Because the ball is higher than normal, you must shorten your grip to avoid hitting the ground behind the ball. For the sake of comfort your hands reach out away from your body a little more. Move your weight onto your toes. You will need to maintain this balance or you will fall back away from the ball on your forward swing. Play your ball back a little for whatever club you're going to use. Because the relative positions in this situation make the plane of your swing flatter, the tendency is to pull or hook a little. Make allowance for this by aiming to the right of your target line.

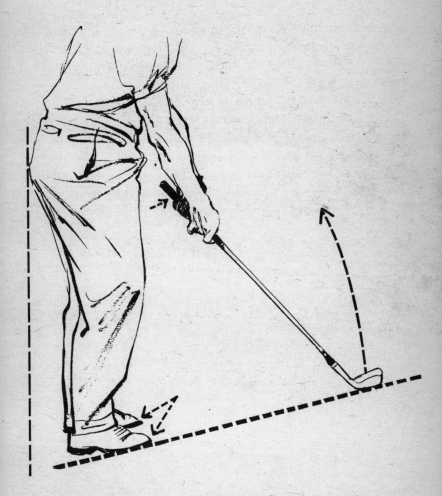

Sidehill lie above your feet: Weight is forward on the toes. Play the ball back and shorten your grip. Aim to the right of the target.

Ball below your feet

This is a condition everyone would like to avoid. Now you must bend your knees and keep your weight back on your heels so as not to tip forward on the forward swing. Move your hands in closer and grip the club at full length. The plane of your swing will be more upright, thus the tendency will be to fade or push (shots flying to the right). Aim a little to the left of your target line. Maintaining good balance and staying down to the ball are the two major efforts here.

Naturally the resulting shot from the hillside lie will usually not be as accurate or as long because of the difficulty in balance and timing. But practice will make them easier.

Sidehill lie below your feet: Weight is back on your heels. Bend your knees and grip the club at full length. Aim to the left of target.

Shanking

As most of you know, a shank is a wild shot which flies off the club to the right. It's caused by striking the ball with the hosel or neck of the club. This action occurs when the club moves out of the plane and away from your body.

The first corrective measure is to be certain that you keep your weight back on your heels at impact. Also clear your mind of the mental picture of shanking. If you keep thinking about shanking you're bound to do it. Take a comfortable, easy shoulder turn on the backswing; hitting with a rigid body without shoulder turn almost forces your swing to the undesired outside plane, with a tendency to move your weight onto your toes. Permit your backswing arc to be upright as it should be, not flat with your clubface open.

Extra speeding up of your clubhead with your arms may cause shanking too. This happens most frequently with short pitch shots when you are trying to get extra crispness or more distance with a short backswing. Any uneven or jerky action invites shanking. Here are two positions particularly vulnerable to shanking: (1) The sidehill lie with your ball below your feet. A shank occurs most often if you try to hit the ball hard. Your weight is inclined to tip forward on your toes causing your clubhead to go into the shanking position. (2) Playing an exaggerated cut shot from a sand trap. The tendency here is to flatten the backswing and lay the clubface open, which almost certainly will throw the clubhead outside too far, causing the shank.

Correct contact.

Contact with the hosel, or neck, produces a shank.

Slicing and hooking

Slicing and hooking are easy. Everyone does it. A beginner can slice or hook without knowing a thing about it. The hard shot to hit is the straight ball. That takes practice, knowledge and time. To be able to slice or hook only when you want to requires a good deal of skill. The slice and the hook are deviations from the straight ball, so first we must look again at how to hit the straight ball. Take a square stance, shoulders square to the line, with your grip and ball in the normal position. With a full shoulder turn you should hit a straight shot. To slice or hook you must alter this normalcy.

Hook

Close your stance—how much depends on how much you want to hook. This turns your plane to a decided inside-out swing. Because you have turned your entire body away from the line you must move the ball back about one or two inches. As you address the ball in this new position you will note that your clubface looks closed when it is aiming straight down the line of flight. The fact that you have moved the ball position back means that your club contacts your ball a bit sooner in the arc of the forward swing, all of which contributes to the sidespin necessary to cause a draw or hook.

By setting your hands, one or both, in a strong position you will exaggerate the closed face at impact and produce a more violent hook. A mild hook, commonly referred to as a draw, can be produced by assuming a normal position so long as your swing comes from the inside out. Sometimes a mild undesired hook can be corrected by simply moving your ball forward an inch or two. The added distance your clubhead has to travel in its arc may be enough to have the angle of the clubface reach your ball square instead of closed.

The hook: Closed stance, inside-out plane, ball position moved forward, clubface comes in closed.

Slice

This is the most common shot in the game, except to control. To hit a fade or slice deliberately, open your stance. Opening your stance automatically shortens your backswing arc and throws the plane of your swing to an outside-in position. Your ball is moved forward a few inches so you are now making contact with the ball at a more forward point of your swinging arc, causing your clubface to be open at impact. The degree of open angle at impact is what must be accurately controlled.

Adjusting one or both hands to a weak position can produce a fade from a square stance or exaggerate a slice from an open stance. The manipulation of these body and hand actions can be altered to produce many different results. These are the shots the pros use to get around trees, bushes and other obstructions. Sometimes the shot works and sometimes it doesn't. This is the danger of learning them; they require exquisite control. As I said before, don't even attempt them unless you can hit a straight shot. Many a golf game has been ruined by golfers trying to learn the fancy stuff before they've learned the basics.

The slice: Open stance, outside-in plane, shortened backswing, ball position moved forward a little, clubface comes in opened.

Chapter 12

SELECTING AND PURCHASING CLUBS

Generalizations for the selection and purchase of clubs are difficult to make. When you are preparing to buy golf equipment seek out your local pro for assistance. One of the reasons I say this is because the finest clubs and golf balls are sold through pro shops. (Both public and private courses have pro shops.) Let's examine a few facts you should be aware of when you go to the local pro.

First there are different degrees of flexibility in the shaft of golf clubs. The stiff-shafted club, one with little give, is best suited to the hard swingers and low handicap players. The other extreme is the whippy or very flexible shaft, more profitable for the older player and women. Then of course there are the shafts with medium give, most recommended for the average golfer. Your build, height, strength, etc., are all factors in deciding which you should use. That's another reason why only a pro can help you.

You are probably already aware that sets of clubs vary as to weight. Again depending on your size, strength, etc., there is one weight just right for you. As we said before, the speed your club is traveling at impact determines the distance your ball will travel. Unless you are physically strong enough to move a heavy club, you will get more distance and control with a lighter club. Select your clubs with something more in mind than just a stick with a hunk of weight on the end of it.

Usually clubs are made with one standard length shaft. However, there are sets available with longer and shorter shafts. Older golfers and shorter players sometimes find longer shafts to their advantage because of the longer arc and distance they produce. Some very tall men choose shorter shafts to gain a more upright swing. Listed below are the degrees of loft for each club. Note the differences; they will give you a good idea of why you have each club.

Clubs	Loft (in degrees)*
Woods One	11
Two	14
Three	16
Four	19
Five	22
Irons Two	21
Three	24
Four	27
Five	31
Six	35
Seven	39
Eight	43
Nine	47
Pitching wedge	51 to 54
Dual wedge (combined pitching and sand wedge)	53 to 54
Sand wedge	55 to 58

* These facings may vary a bit according to each manufacturer.

Do not adjust the posture of your body for each club. In other words don't stand more erect for the longer clubs or stoop for the short clubs. All matched clubs are designed to adjust this action for you. As the club shortens, your hands move in closer to your body. This is where the adjustment is made.

The distance you normally get from each club is something you should know. On the course you must be able to make some kind of mental estimate of the distance of your next shot. The score card provides a good clue although it is not always accurate. If you are playing a 380-yard hole and you know you drive 210 yards, then you have 170 yards to go. Other aids in estimating distances on a course you've already played are trees, traps, rocks, etc., from which

154

you can judge by previous experience. Make it your business to practice with each of your clubs to learn your distances with all their variations. Through experience I know my distances quite accurately. I could vary these distances but I do not choose to stretch them out very much. I let the club do the work. If I have to add 10 or 20 yards to what I consider normal, I take a longer club. Hitting harder than normal usually sacrifices accuracy. My advice to you is: take the extra club. Golf isn't a game of who can hit the farthest; it's getting in the hole in the fewest strokes that counts.

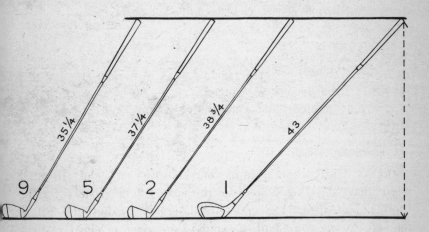

All matched sets of clubs are made so that, when properly soled, the upper ends of the shafts of each club will form a line parallel to the ground. This permits you to take the same position with every club, regardless of the length of club you may choose for any shot.

The sole of your club should lie flat on the ground.

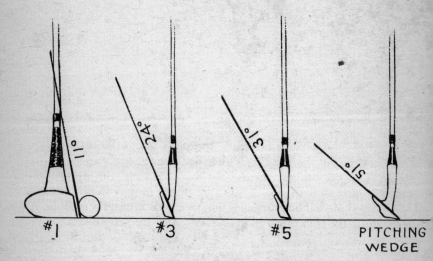

Comparative loft of four clubs.

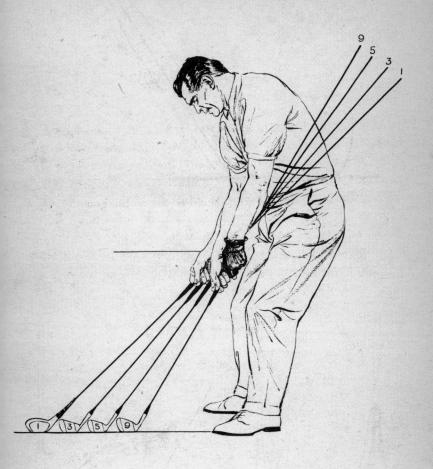

The erectness of your body remains the same with all lengths of clubs. As the length of the club shortens, your hands move in closer to your body.

Well, that's about it from this end.

What happens now is up to you. If you learn and practice the mechanics as presented in this book, you're on your way to an exciting rediscovery of golf. As for me, I'm going out to practice and play a round. There are a lot of tournaments coming up and, God willing, I'll be in there trying to win that big money. My family will live better if I do and maybe I can do some more fishing. I don't like working too much so this is the next best thing. It's been a real pleasure for me, with Lea's help, to have been able to pass this information along to you. I know it will do a lot for your game.